Fact Finders™

Biographies

Duke Ellington

Jazz Composer

by Judy Monroe

Consultant:
John Edward Hasse
Curator of American Music
Smithsonian Institution
Washington, D.C.

Capstone *press*
Mankato, Minnesota

Fact Finders is published by Capstone Press,
151 Good Counsel Drive, P.O. Box 669, Mankato, Minnesota 56002.
www.capstonepress.com

Library of Congress Cataloging-in-Publication Data
Monroe, Judy.
    Duke Ellington: jazz composer / by Judy Monroe.
    p. cm.—(Fact finders. Biographies)
    Includes bibliographical references and index.
    ISBN 0-7368-3741-8 (hardcover)
    1. Ellington, Duke, 1899–1974—Juvenile literature. 2. Jazz musicians—United
States—Biography—Juvenile literature. I. Title. II. Series.
ML3930.E44M59 2005
781.65'092—dc22   2004011302

Summary: An introduction to the life of African American musician Duke Ellington,
    who influenced jazz and popular music.

Editorial Credits
Megan Schoeneberger, editor; Juliette Peters, set designer; Patrick D. Dentinger, book
    designer and illustrator; Kelly Garvin, photo researcher; Scott Thoms, photo editor

Photo Credits
AP/Wide World Photos, 26
Archives Center, National Museum of American History, Behring Center, Smithsonian
    Institution/Duke Ellington Collection, 7, 14, 16–17, 21
Corbis, 9; Bettmann, 5, 10–11, 18, 23, 24–25; Ted Williams, 22
Courtesy of the Louisiana State Museum, 12
Getty Images Inc./Hulton Archive, cover, 1, 19, 27
Library of Congress, 15

1 2 3 4 5 6 10 09 08 07 06 05

Table of Contents

A Jazzy Birthday

On April 29, 1969, the king of jazz came to the White House. He was Duke Ellington, and it was his 70th birthday.

More than 100 people came to honor Ellington. He greeted his friends with four kisses, two on each cheek. After dinner, President Richard Nixon gave Ellington the Medal of Freedom for his long career. People clapped and cheered.

Next came music. Nixon started by playing "Happy Birthday" on the piano. Then a band played Ellington's jazz music. Around midnight, the president went to bed. But the musicians stayed. Ellington sat down at the piano and played past 2:00 in the morning.

President Richard Nixon (right) presented the Medal of Freedom to Duke Ellington.

King of Jazz

Ellington was the king of jazz, a type of music with strong **rhythm**. Players make up tunes and add notes in unexpected places. Ellington played piano and wrote jazz for his own band.

Childhood

Edward Kennedy Ellington was born April 29, 1899. His parents were James and Daisy Ellington. His younger sister, Ruth, was born in 1915. The family lived in Washington, D.C., where Ellington's father worked for the U.S. Navy. He also sometimes worked at the White House as a waiter.

Ellington's parents raised him to be proud that he was African American. His mother told him many times, "You are blessed." Ellington learned African American history from his parents and from teachers at school.

Ellington posed for this photograph when he was 6 years old.

Umpy-Dump Music

Ellington's parents played the piano. They wanted their son to play too. While in grade school, Ellington took piano lessons. Mrs. Clinkscales was his teacher. He did not like his lessons. The music had the same slow one-and-two and one-and-two rhythm. He called it umpy-dump music. He soon stopped playing the piano.

Ellington loved baseball and played the game with other boys. He also liked to watch baseball. He got a job at a baseball park selling gum, candy, and popcorn.

The Washington Senators baseball team played at Griffith Stadium, where Ellington sold treats.

In school, Ellington liked art the best. He was good at drawing and painting. He won a poster contest. He began to think about becoming an artist to make money.

FACT!

Ellington believed the 13th day of the month was lucky. When the 13th fell on a Friday, Ellington believed the day was especially lucky.

Choosing Music

In high school, Ellington was graceful and well mannered. A friend called him Duke because of his polite ways. The name stuck.

Ellington played pool with friends after school. At one pool hall, famous African American musicians came to play pool and the piano. They played new music called **ragtime**.

Ellington liked this music. He tried to play ragtime on the piano. At first, Ellington did not play well. He kept practicing for hours every day. In 1914, Ellington wrote his first song. He called it the "Soda Fountain Rag."

As a teenager, Ellington learned to play the piano very well.

Learning about Jazz

Ellington needed a piano teacher. He found Oliver "Doc" Perry, a popular Washington bandleader. Perry often came to the pool hall. He taught Ellington how to read music and play ragtime and jazz.

The Original Dixieland Jazz Band made the first jazz recording. Ellington learned from listening to bands like this one.

Ellington loved jazz music. In the early 1900s, jazz was a new type of American music. It is lively and full of twists and turns. It uses tricky rhythms. Jazz musicians often make up parts of the music while they are playing.

Perry helped Ellington find jobs. Ellington played at dances and restaurants. He also played background music for a magician.

Art or Music?

In his free time, Ellington worked on his art. In 1916, Ellington won a big art prize. He could pay for art school with the money he won.

Ellington thought about what to do. Should he study art or music? He was already making money playing music. He decided to quit high school to look for music jobs.

Ellington formed a small band, the Duke's Serenaders. Ellington played the piano and wrote music. Others in his band played the drums, banjo, trumpet, and sax.

Ellington (center) sits with members of the Duke's Serenaders.

Ellington placed an ad in the telephone book. He listed himself as **manager** of the band. Soon, the Duke's Serenaders had jobs playing all over Washington, D.C.

Ellington now had enough money for a family. On July 2, 1918, he married Edna Thompson. Their son, Mercer, was born March 11, 1919. Ellington bought a house for his new family.

Ellington's neighbor was Henry Grant. Grant was a music teacher. Ellington took lessons from Grant twice a week. Ellington learned about **harmony** and African American music.

⬆ Ellington played his first show in this building known as True Reformers Hall in Washington, D.C. Duron Paints bought the building in 1959. It became a historic landmark in the 1980s.

FACT!

Ellington barely passed his high school music class. He earned a D grade.

New York

In 1923, Ellington and his band moved to Harlem. Harlem is part of New York City. Many famous African American writers, musicians, and artists lived in Harlem in the early 1900s.

The band was now called the Washingtonians. They played in clubs. Ellington and his band began making records. Soon, people heard the Washingtonians on the radio.

Top Spot

In 1927, Ellington's band got a job at the Cotton Club. It was Harlem's top nightclub. The band played two shows a night.

Ellington (far right) and
the Washingtonians played
many shows in New York.

Ellington's band grew to 12 players.
He called this new band Duke Ellington
and His Orchestra. Ellington's career
took off. In 1931, he took his band across
the United States. In 1932 and 1939, they
went to Europe.

▲ Ellington wrote
music wherever
and whenever
he could.

Ellington wrote music for his
band. He jotted ideas on envelopes
and scraps of paper. His songs
brought out each player's strengths
and hid any weaknesses. The band
sometimes played the music note for
note. Other times, Ellington told the
players to play the music they felt.

QUOTE

"The most important
thing I look for in a
musician is whether he
knows how to listen."
—Duke Ellington

Billy Strayhorn

In 1939, Ellington met Billy Strayhorn. Strayhorn was a **composer** and piano player. He wrote many new songs for Ellington's band. One of his biggest hits was "Take the 'A' Train." The band recorded it in 1941. Ellington and Strayhorn also wrote music together. Their friendship lasted until Strayhorn died in 1967.

Meanwhile, a new type of jazz became the craze. **Swing** was a light, fast dance sound. Ellington added more swing to his music. People all over danced to Ellington's new sounds.

▲ Ellington (left) and Strayhorn (right) often wrote songs together. Ellington sometimes jotted notes on his shirt cuff to remember them.

FACT!

Ellington owned more than 150 suits and 1,000 neckties. Not one of them was green. He hated the color green.

19

On Top

On January 23, 1943, Duke Ellington and His Orchestra played at Carnegie Hall in New York City. Ellington wrote a long piece of music called "Black, Brown, and Beige" to play. This music tells the history of African Americans in America. "Black" was about people in everyday life. "Brown" honored soldiers in wars. "Beige" was about the music of Harlem.

Low Notes and High Notes

In the 1950s, many people lost interest in jazz and swing. Ellington did not write much music. The band did not make a great deal of money. Some people thought Ellington and his band were finished.

DUKE ELLINGTON AND HIS ORCHESTRA

Twentieth Anniversary Concert

CARNEGIE HALL
New York

Saturday Evening, January 23, 1943
at 8:45 o'clock

Proceeds for Russian War Relief

P R O G R A M

I.

Black and Tan Fantasy	*Ellington-Miley*
Rockin' in Rhythm	*Ellington-Carney*
Blue Serge	*Mercer Ellington*
Jumpin' Punkins	*Mercer Ellington*

II.

Ellington

Portrait of Bert Williams
Portrait of Bojangles
Portrait of Florence Mills

III.

Ellington

Black, Brown and Beige
(A Tone Parallel to the History of the Negro in America.)

— Intermission —

IV.

Ellington

The Flaming Sword

Billy Strayhorn

Dirge
Nocturne
Stomp

V.

Ellington

Are You Stickin'? .... *Tizol*
(Chauncey Haughton, clarinet)

Bakiff .... *Ellington*
(Juan Tizol, valve trombone; Ray Nance, violin)

Jack the Bear .... *Ellington*
(Alvin Raglin, string bass)

Blue Belles of Harlem .... *Ellington*
(Duke Ellington, piano)

Cotton Tail .... *Ellington*
(Ben Webster, tenor saxophone)

Day Dream .... *Ellington-Strayhorn*
(Johnny Hodges, alto saxophone)

Rose of the Rio Grande .... *Warren-Gorman-Leslie*
(Lawrence Brown, trombone)

Trumpet in Spades .... *Ellington*
(Rex Stewart, cornet)

VI.

Ellington

Don't Get Around Much Any More
Goin' Up
Mood Indigo

*(Duke Ellington and his orchestra are under the exclusive
management of the William Morris Agency, Inc.)*

A program from Ellington's first performance at Carnegie Hall lists the songs the band played that night.

Ellington did not give up. In July 1956, Ellington led his band at the Newport Jazz Festival in Rhode Island. That night, sax player Paul Gonsalves let loose with 27 **choruses** in a row. The crowd went wild. They danced and cheered.

The whole country soon heard about the Ellington band's show at the festival. Then, Ellington's picture was on the cover of *Time* magazine on August 29, 1956. The king of jazz and his band were back on top.

Paul Gonsalves' saxophone solo at the Newport Jazz Festival lifted Ellington's band back into the spotlight.

Around the World

In 1963, the U.S. State Department asked Ellington and his band to tour around the world. The band went to the Middle East, Europe, Japan, Russia, and South America. Tickets sold fast. Ellington often wrote new music for each place.

As Ellington grew older, he turned to religious music. He wrote three long pieces for jazz bands to play in large churches. He called them **sacred** concerts.

▲ Ellington and his band played a sacred concert at the Cathedral of St. John the Divine in New York City.

QUOTE

"I'm a telephone freak. [It's] the greatest invention since peanut brittle."
　　　　—Duke Ellington

A Jazz Legacy

In the 1960s, Ellington's son Mercer joined the band. He played trumpet and managed the band.

In Ellington's later years, he lost some of his longtime band players. Some died, and others left to play in other bands. Ellington always found new players. The band sounded a little different, but Ellington still kept writing music.

Ellington also kept getting awards. He won 13 Grammy Awards. He received special degrees from 19 schools. Four presidents asked Ellington to the White House.

Ellington and his band won two Grammy Awards in 1967.

In 1973, Ellington became ill with lung cancer. He grew sick and weak. On May 24, 1974, Ellington died. More than 12,000 people came to his funeral in New York to say good-bye to the king of jazz.

A Jazz Great

Ellington was a great jazz piano player and composer. When Ellington heard new sounds, he wove them into his music. He wrote about 2,000 pieces of music.

Many people think Ellington is the most important person in jazz. Small and large groups still play his music. People still sing his songs. People love to hear Ellington's music.

Fast Facts

Full name: Edward Kennedy Ellington

Occupation: Composer, bandleader, and pianist

Birth: April 29, 1899

Death: May 24, 1974

Hometown: Washington, D.C.

Parents: James Edward and Daisy Kennedy Ellington

Sister: Ruth Ellington

Wife: Edna Thompson Ellington

Son: Mercer Ellington

Education: Completed 11th grade; little formal music education

Major awards:

13 Grammy Awards

President's Gold Medal, 1966

Presidential Medal of Freedom, 1969

Big Band and Jazz Hall of Fame, 1978

Time Line

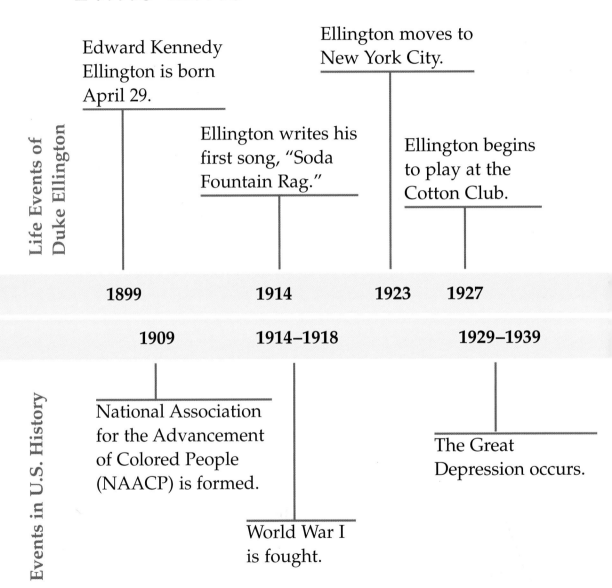

Life Events of Duke Ellington

Edward Kennedy Ellington is born April 29.

Ellington writes his first song, "Soda Fountain Rag."

Ellington moves to New York City.

Ellington begins to play at the Cotton Club.

1899   1914   1923   1927

1909   1914–1918   1929–1939

Events in U.S. History

National Association for the Advancement of Colored People (NAACP) is formed.

World War I is fought.

The Great Depression occurs.

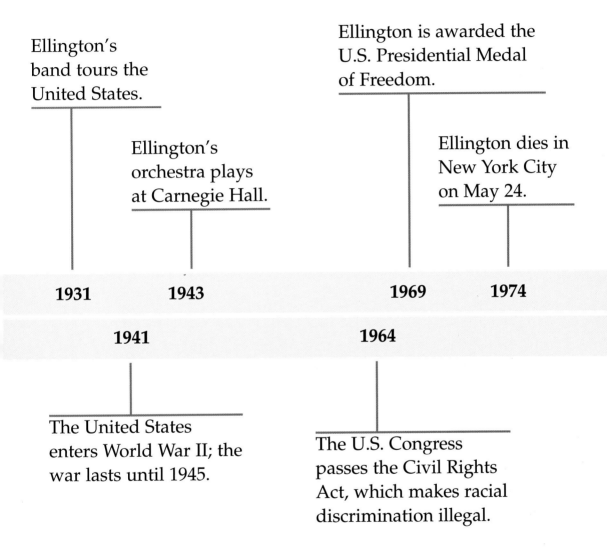

Ellington's band tours the United States.

Ellington's orchestra plays at Carnegie Hall.

Ellington is awarded the U.S. Presidential Medal of Freedom.

Ellington dies in New York City on May 24.

1931   **1943**   **1969**   **1974**

1941   **1964**

The United States enters World War II; the war lasts until 1945.

The U.S. Congress passes the Civil Rights Act, which makes racial discrimination illegal.

Glossary

chorus (KOR-uhss)—the part of a song that is repeated after each verse

composer (kuhm-POZE-ur)—a writer of music

harmony (HAR-muh-nee)—a set of musical notes played at the same time; the notes blend together to form harmony.

manager (MAN-uh-jur)—a person in charge of a group; a band's manager schedules performances and arranges transportation.

ragtime (RAG-time)—an early type of jazz with a strong rhythm; ragtime was especially popular from 1890 to 1915.

rhythm (RITH-uhm)—a regular beat in music

sacred (SAY-krid)—holy, or having to do with religion

swing (SWING)—a style of lively jazz music originally played by large dance bands in the 1930s

Internet Sites

FactHound offers a safe, fun way to find Internet sites related to this book. All of the sites on FactHound have been researched by our staff.

Here's how:

1. Visit *www.facthound.com*
2. Type in this special code **0736837418** for age-appropriate sites. Or enter a search word related to this book for a more general search.
3. Click on the **Fetch It** button.

FactHound will fetch the best sites for you!

Read More

Bankston, John. *The Life and Times of Duke Ellington.* Masters of Music. Hockessin, Del.: Mitchell Lane Publishers, 2005.

Brown, Gene. *Duke Ellington: Jazz Master.* Giants of Art and Culture. Woodbridge, Conn.: Blackbirch Press, 2001.

Terrill, Richard. *Duke Ellington.* African American Biographies. Chicago: Raintree, 2003.

Index